No, It's Just You

*A Memoir in 58 One-Act Plays
And One Montage*

By Andrew Saulters
With Various Collaborators

Scuppernong Editions   Greensboro

Text in Baskerville.

ISBN 978-1-7329328-1-4

Scuppernong Editions offers the occasional
publication of adventuresome, commercially
questionable writing in all genres.

Scuppernong Editions
304 South Elm Street
Greensboro, NC 27401

No, It's Just You

No, It's Just You

Andrew Saulters and the Finding of Fact

[County courthouse, lazy Monday morning. ANDREW SAULTERS has been preliminarily selected as Juror No. 12 in a personal injury civil case. He sits in the wood-rail jury box in the wood-paneled courtroom as the PROSECUTING ATTORNEY interviews the candidates in series.]

PROSECUTING ATTORNEY. [Makes note on grid of Post-It Notes indicating jury candidates. Addresses JUROR 9.] Ms. ———, do you have a favorite TV show?

JUROR 9. I like "Orange is the New Black."

P.A. Thank you. [Makes note. Addresses JUROR 10.] And Ms. ———, do you like to watch anything on TV?

JUROR 10. "True Detective," "True Blood."

P.A. Thank you. [Makes note. Addresses JUROR 11.] Mr. ———, do you have a favorite TV show?

JUROR 11. I like the Golf Channel.

P.A. Thank you. [Makes note. Addresses ANDREW SAULTERS.] Mr. Saulters, do you have a favorite TV show?

ANDREW SAULTERS. No, I can honestly say I do not. I don't watch TV.

P.A. [Reviews notes.] Well, you say you teach English. Do you have a particular part of your class that you most like teaching?

A.S. Argument. And persuasion.

P.A. You look forward to that?

A.S. Sure.

P.A. Would you say you teach that part better than any other?

A.S. No, I wouldn't say so.

P.A. You teach it all pretty well, then, would you say?

A.S. No, I don't know if I would say that, either.

P.A. [Makes note.] Thank you.

Andrew Saulters and the Negative Dialectic

[Greensboro. An anonymous coffeeshop on the outskirts of town. ANDREW SAULTERS begins to set up his considerable writing equipage when a GARRULOUS BARISTA hails him.]

GARRULOUS BARISTA. Hey man, I just wanted to ask you how the music's going.

ANDREW SAULTERS. Excuse me?

G.B. How's it going, playing music?

A.S. I don't play music.

G.B. You were playing music when I saw you last time.

A.S. That wasn't me. I don't play music.

G.B. But you were carrying a guitar with you, playing gigs—

A.S. Who do you think I am?

G.B. [Blinking, pausing.] I don't know. You were with Morgan....

A.S. What is Morgan's last name?

G.B. Morgan McP———, a barista here.

A.S. I don't know Morgan McP———, a barista here.

G.B. You come in here a lot, wearing your hat...

A.S. I haven't been in here for two weeks. The last time before that was three years ago.

G.B. [Focused silence.]

A.S. [Produces list written on the back of a business card.] Look at this. It's a list of all the people for whom I've been confused.

G.B. Huh.

A.S. See that guy, "Todd." No, not that Todd. The third one. Someone here mistook me for him three years ago.

G.B. I'll tell you who you look like.

4

A.S. Maybe you thought I was G——— M———. Got a hat, guitar, long hair. Right there, middle column. "G——— M———." I don't see the resemblance, but, you know.

G.B. You look like Felix Cavaliere.

A.S. Who's Felix Cavaliere?

G.B. You don't know who Felix Cavaliere is.

A.S. No.

G.B. Felix Cavaliere, singer, songwriter, producer and musician renowned for his work with The Rascals?

A.S. Don't know him.

G.B. [Hands card back.] Yep. Look just like him.

Andrew Saulters and the Benefit of the Doubt

[Early morning, crisp air. As he bicycles to school, ANDREW SAULTERS is passed by a bus filled with elementary school students who giggle as they peer at him through the rear windows of the vehicle. One STUDENT, smiling broadly, glances cursorily about before opening his window and projecting his head through it. A.S. braces for a withering taunt or projectile.]

STUDENT. [While bus turns right, bifurcating from the route A.S. continues upon.] You all right?

Andrew Saulters and the Waitress at the End of Time

[Evening, after stormy weather in Phenix City, AL. ANDREW SAULTERS and PARENTS take dinner at a restaurant offering pancakes variously developed from the national cuisines of Northern European countries. A BESPECTACLED WAITRESS, gray-haired and short, approaches for the drink order.]

BESPECTACLED WAITRESS. What will you have?
MOTHER. Water, no ice, no lemon.

[FATHER looks at A.S., who nods back at him.]

FATHER. Water, please.
A.S. Water for me.

[B.W. departs, but returns after a few steps.]

B.W. I'm coming back. [Looking at A.S.] I thought you were gone.
A.S. [Confused about waitress.] Where did I go?
B.W. I thought you went away, out of state.
A.S. I did go away, out of state.
B.W. You got old.
A.S. I did get old. [Cheerful tone.] Going to get older!
B.W. You got older.

[B.W. departs.]

Andrew Saulters and the Life of the Mind

[Night at the coffeeshop counter. ANDREW SAULTERS drafts correspondences on his mobile laptop computer, the looseleaf pages of a manuscript beside him. Having just rediscovered that well-known tool of pseudoscience, the Enneagram Model of Personality, SAULTERS remembers he is a: five. Five, fiver, fivo, he thinks, aware that excessive introspection is itself a premiere activity of fives. A SECOND COFFEESHOP PATRON approaches the counter.]

SECOND COFFEESHOP PATRON. [To BARISTA on duty.] Do you have a—

[S.C.P. scans the counter and picks up the first page of the manuscript, its table of contents, which lies face-down beside A.S. S.C.P. studies it. A.S. watches him, waits. The BARISTA is not sure what to do. S.C.P. continues to study the table of contents. A.S. waits, indicates excitement to B. via facial gesture.]

BARISTA. [Taking table of contents from S.C.P.] That's not a menu—
S.C.P. Oh!
A.S. [In head.] Oh.

Carpe Diem, Andrew Saulters

[Sidewalk on a mild afternoon. ANDREW SAULTERS locks his bike. A WOMAN walks a DOG and chats to a FRIEND. SAULTERS mouths the word "hello" to the DOG, who does not regard him. After passing SAULTERS, WOMAN WITH DOG turns about and hails him.]

WOMAN WITH DOG. You look like Robin Williams, from "Dead Poets Society," today!

[A.S. smiles, perhaps too much, on purpose. The sun is in his eyes. The two women acquire postures of confusion. DOG pulls against the leash gently, purposelessly.]

W.W.D. I mean. You look just like Robin Williams, in that role!
FRIEND OF WOMAN WITH DOG. Take it as a compliment!
W.W.D. It's a compliment!
F.O.W.W.D. She means it as a compliment!

[Exeunt WOMAN WITH DOG, FRIEND OF WOMAN WITH DOG, DOG.]

Andrew Saulters and Every Negative Thing
Ten Miles Down the Road

[Evening, bookstore. ANDREW SAULTERS is making for the exit when he notices how the fold in the BOOKSHOP CLERK's collar has strayed from the crisp meridian between base and leaf, a jarring dissonance in the impeccable style of the clerk. He corrects the orientation of the collar without first announcing the nature of his enterprise, then clicks his tongue and makes the OK gesture. When he attempts to leave he is hailed by BOOKSTORE PATRONS conversing with the CLERK.]

BOOKSTORE PATRON 1. Robin Williams!

ANDREW SAULTERS. I'm sorry?

BOOKSTORE PATRON 2. [Spouse of B.P. 1.] You look just like Robin Williams!

A.S. Oh really?

BOOKSTORE CLERK. This is not the first time he's heard that.

B.P. 1. It's very much your look.

A.S. [Shifts weight to one foot, coquettishly placing hands on hips, employing a rising intonation pattern.] Which movie?

B.C. Probably "Dead Poet's Society."

B.P. 1. [Not entirely sure what's happening.] Yeah, "Dead Poet's Society." [B.P. 2 smiles, nods.]

A.S. I prefer "Good Will Hunting." The cynicism, the loss of hope.

B.P. 1. [Missing no beats at all.] You look good! A lot younger!

A.S. And also not dead!

B.P. 1. Thankfully!

Andrew Saulters and the Longest Haul

[Morning; classroom. In an attempt to dissuade his students from going long without proper sleep, ANDREW SAULTERS discourses upon a time he stayed up for five days in an effort to make hall decorations for summer camp students, only to produce irremediably subpar results.]

ANDREW SAULTERS. It goes without saying, of course, that sleep deprivation or no, pairing patent illustrations with quotations from world literature is a terrible plan for door decorations.

STUDENT 1. So, did you fall out after that?

A.S. No, after that the kids came and it was time to do the work, so I did it.

STUDENT 2. It sounds like you just wasted five days of your life!

A.S. Oh, my friend. I've wasted more than that.

Andrew Saulters and the State of the Art

[Coffeeshop: a bright Sunday morning. ANDREW SAULTERS is attempting a poem in the window seat. A man approaches him to ask a question about a conversation that occurred not long ago, but hangs back, observing his exertions. Ultimately, there is no stopping inquiry, and the HESITANT INTERLOCUTOR speaks.]

HESITANT INTERLOCUTOR. Andrew.

ANDREW SAULTERS. [Head down, directing the full force of his unproductive creative powers.] Yes.

H.I. Who was that first poet you mentioned?

A.S. [Looking at page.] First poet.

H.I. The first one in English. The illiterate one who was moved to write by a vision from God.

A.S. [Still looking at page.] Caedmon.

H.I. Caedmon?

A.S. [Looking at page.] Caedmon.

H.I. *C-A—*

A.S. [Looks vacantly outside.] *C-A-E-D-M-O-N.*

H.I. *C-A-E-D-M-O-N?*

A.S. Yes.

H.I. Thanks.

[HESITANT INTERLOCUTOR departs. SAULTERS stares at the page.]

Andrew Saulters, Child of God

[A cool evening in downtown Greensboro. Passed now below the horizon, the sun has left nearly no color in the sky. ANDREW SAULTERS leans against a light post clipping his fingernails. An INTERLOCUTOR clad in a light coat and backward cap eagerly confides to him a plan.]

EAGER INTERLOCUTOR. So, what we have to do is get evil to bite the apple like Eve bit the apple, right?

ANDREW SAULTERS. [Pauses.] Sure.

E.I. We have to get these clubs shut down.

A.S. Which clubs?

E.I. [Gesturing up the street.] All of these clubs, up on Greene Street and Elm.

A.S. Oh, I see.

E.I. If we keep the kids out of these clubs, for a whole year, then evil won't be able to get at them, right?

A.S. [Looks up the street.]

E.I. Right? Are you for the kids?

A.S. Oh, yes. I'm for the kids.

E.I. Then we need to keep 'em out of the clubs, and they'll shut down. We've got to spread the word, right?

A.S. [Straightens up, stepping away from light post. Looks at E.I.]

E.I. Right? I was walking up the street there, and I was told to spread this message. I am a Child Son of God.

A.S. Hey, now. We're all children of God.

E.I. No, I'm the Jesus Christ Child Son of God. We're going to spread the word, right?

A.S. [Looks into E.I.'s eyes silently. E.I. looks straight at him but not into his eyes.]

E.I. If we spread the word, all the parents and all the kids and the council members will stay out of the clubs, and after a year, they'll shut down. Right? Then I'll walk into that council room with Jesus and the Holy Spirit and sit down, and I'll tell them my plan. We've got to get evil to bite the apple just like Eve did, right?

A.S. [Looks past E.I., up the block.]

E.I. You with me?

A.S. [Extending hand for a farewell handshake.] I'm with you. Good luck.

E.I. [Accepting handshake.] We don't need any luck if we get the kids to stay out of the clubs. You're going to spread the word?

A.S. I will spread the word.

E.I. [Looking into the sky.] Just don't mention the clubs. Leave the clubs out of it.

A.S. [Bobbing his hand in E.I.'s light grip to suggest he would like to terminate the handshake.] All right.

E.I. You catch my drift?

A.S. [Bobbing hand again.] I've got it. No clubs. I'll tell everyone. It was nice meeting you. What's your name?

E.I. I don't go by my earthly name, don't go by my Social Security number.

A.S. I see. Is there a name you call yourself by?

E.I. I'm the Jesus Child Son of God. [Pausing, looking past A.S. at storefront containing club.] I'm also called The Red Machine.

14

A.S. [Touches E.I.'s hand with his other hand. Introduces himself.] It was nice meeting you.

E.I. [Releases handshake.] You'll spread the word?

A.S. [Stepping away.] I will spread it.

E.I. Hey.

A.S. [Turning about.]

E.I. [Advancing, speaking in low voice.] Put it on the internet.

A.S. Okay, I will.

E.I. [Looks away, at the sky.] Put it on Facebook.

A.S. Got it.

E.I. Do you get my drift?

A.S. I hear you.

Do Unto Others, Thou Andrew Saulters

[ANDREW SAULTERS waits for the signal at Tate and Lee to change. An EARNEST FELLOW approaches and addresses him from the adjacent lane.]

EARNEST FELLOW. You look like Jesus Christ.

ANDREW SAULTERS. Excuse me?

E.F. [Takes off hat and bows slightly, cupping hands as if in prayer.] You look like Jesus Christ.

A.S. I am not him.

E.F. You look like him.

A.S. [Shrugs.]

E.F. Can you drive me to Wendy's?

Andrew Saulters and Vox Conscientiae

[Exterior: an Italian restaurant, afternoon. ANDREW SAULTERS has just concluded lunch with his teaching colleagues and they are about to resume fall semester orientation. Unseen, a colleague's YOUNG CHILD creeps up behind SAULTERS and addresses him in his great, booming seven-year-old voice.]

YOUNG CHILD. *This is your conscience!*
ANDREW SAULTERS. [Pantomiming shock, he regards the sky.] My! It's been a while since I heard from you!
Y.C. *I am here now, I am your conscience!*
A.S. Well, yes. What do you say, Conscience?
Y.C. *You should drink more soda!*
A.S. But I gave up soda three years ago!
Y.C. *You should steal it from the restaurant!*
A.S. Conscience, that's a terrible idea!
Y.C. *You should drink soda now!*
A.S. I'll be seeing you later, Conscience.

[SAULTERS departs.]

Y.C. But wait!

[SAULTERS waves, as one might if embarking for summer camp.]

Andrew Saulters and the Value of College

[A bell tower announces noon through the classroom's open window. ANDREW SAULTERS invites his students to partake in grandiose and freewheeling discussion on the purpose of a college education.]

ANDREW SAULTERS. Pray tell me, pupils, why go to college?

STUDENT 1. Well, when I started, I was after the money, but I'm still thinking about that.

A.S. Yes, I see! though that was not my quarry as an undergraduate. Except, perhaps, it ought have been—why else should one study engineering?

STUDENT 1. Oh, yeah. I forgot you did that.

A.S. Indeed. Do you know why I did that?

STUDENT 1. No.

A.S. I thought planes were beautiful. I remember it well. I missed my very first class on my very first day in college. I tracked down the professor and upon locating him, I cried out, "Professor! Forgive me, I have missed your class!" He invited me to partake in small talk with him, saying, "Come, let us discourse as I return to my office." As we walked, he asked, "What is it you are studying?" "Aerospace engineering," I said. "Why aerospace engineering?" he asked. "Because I think planes are beautiful," I said. "The way they fly is beautiful." "You might want to change your field of study," he said. It took me four and a half years to realize what he meant.

STUDENT 2. Four years!

A.S. Four and a half years.

STUDENT 2. Four and a half years!

A.S. Indeed.

[Silence.]

STUDENT 1. But you teach English.

A.S. Yes. I turned down NASA to study poetry in graduate school. They wanted me to work on controls stuff for the Space Shuttle. That's the stuff that tells the autopilot what to do. I probably would have been out a job by now if I had stuck with them. Who knows.

[Silence.]

STUDENT 2. Have you ever thought about using that degree?

A.S. [In head: Do you mean to say I ought?] No.

Andrew Saulters and the Angel of History

[Twilight: Union Street and 2nd Avenue. Sidewalks are filling with the fashionable young professionals of Seattle. ANDREW SAULTERS, attired in mismatched coat and hat, is searching for a place to write. He waits at a crosswalk, and a NEWSPAPER SALESMAN addresses him.]

NEWSPAPER SALESMAN. That's a nice hat!

ANDREW SAULTERS. Thanks.

N.S. [Gestures with paper in hand.] Hey, you want a paper!

A.S. [Glances at paper, waves hand.] No, thanks.

[N.S. begins a follow-up pitch, but he is forced to delay it by a cough. He beats his chest to recuperate.]

N.S. [Leaning toward A.S., newspaper in hand.] That's old age!

[A.S. tries to produce a reply at once witty and sincere. He cannot. A.S. feels old and has felt so for a while, but everyone feels old, he thinks. In his idleness, A.S. utters a long, undistinguished syllable before the light changes and he proceeds across the street.]

N.S. [Shouting as A.S. continues away.] Hey, you're not even smart!

[A.S. reaches the other side of the street and continues to walk away without turning back.]

N.S. [Shouting with greater intensity.] You're not smart!

[A young man and woman walking beside A.S. quietly comment between themselves on the commotion.]

N.S. [Shouting still, quite distant.] I can tell by the way you dress!

A.S. [Walking, looking straight ahead.] That's true. I mean to say, I guess that's true.

Andrew Saulters and Tunnel Vision

[Night, sidewalk. ANDREW SAULTERS leaves the coffeeshop because the coffeeshop must close. His waking thought had been that today, by sheer chance, could be his last day on earth. Okay, he had said. Thereafter, he was at peace in the morning commute and in his classes and in his tutoring session about the normal distribution curve. Sometime in the evening this ease had yielded to the familiar sense that soon the day would end before enough had been done, as many days had ended, would end. Beside his bicycle, a WOMAN WITH BAGS, also recently departed from the coffeeshop, loads her equipage into a shopping cart. He approaches in order to load the bicycle and make for another place to work.]

WOMAN WITH BAGS. [Looking up as ANDREW SAULTERS loads his
    bicycle.] I'm sorry.
ANDREW SAULTERS. It's okay.
W.W.B. Are you homeless?
A.S. No.
W.W.B. [Considers him briefly.] Have you ever been homeless?
A.S. [Considers himself.] No, ma'am.

[Exeunt in opposite directions, SAULTERS and WOMAN WITH BAGS.]

22

Andrew Saulters and the Fifth Type of Ambiguity

[Afternoon, windowless classroom. Students brainstorm toward their final portfolios on the question of what challenges they have faced as readers, writers, or thinkers in the class. ANDREW SAULTERS watches, a study of vigilance. Time is up.]

ANDREW SAULTERS. Would anyone like to share a challenge they've experienced? I mean, apart from, like, "Andrew Saulters' voice was terribly monotonous. Each class was a struggle against oblivion." I'm already aware that was a challenge.

[STUDENT raises hand.]

A.S. Yes, ———?

S. Sometimes, in conferences, you'd do this thing where you wouldn't tell me whether what I was doing was good or bad, you just kind of said things about it, like, describing what it was doing.

A.S. Yes?

S. And it was never directed toward saying it was needing to be fixed. It was hard to get an idea about whether it was good or bad.

A.S. And this was difficult?

S. Yes.

A.S. That could be a great topic to consider in your portfolio—but in what ways does that relate to something that's bigger than the class, something that's not just an artifact of school? You might wish to discuss that in terms of the difficulty of determining what is actually saying what you need it to say and what is not—or the difficulty of determining whether something really needs to say what you think it needs to say. Does that sound related to that?

s. Yes.

A.S. Or you might choose to think of that in the broader terms of your own writing and revising process. What do you think you would do with this topic?

s. I'm not sure yet. I thought I would bring it up because it might be something to write about?

A.S. Okay. You might be able to discuss that from the angle of engaging with different styles of peer review, too. Does that make sense? [Pause.] Wait a moment. Wait. Am I doing that thing right now? The thing where I don't say whether something is good or bad, but I just talk about it? Am I doing that right now?

s. [Nods in terror.]

A.S. [In head.] But what of the myth of pure description?

Andrew Saulters and the Expressive Powers of Language

[Afternoon, coffeeshop. ANDREW SAULTERS, enmired in the style guide and dictionary that are the editor's unwieldy instruments, is querying a manuscript. He finds a new word that pleases him and fetches himself to the first person who will hear the news.]

ANDREW SAULTERS Ah! There's a word for the scar of a healed head wound!

BARISTA. [Clearly bewildered.] There's a word for the scar...?

A.S. Of a healed...

B. Of a healed head...

A.S. Wound.

B. Wound?

A.S. There's a word for the scar of a healed head wound!

B. Well, what is it?

A.S. "Cicatrix."

B. [Says the word, uncertain.] How's it spelled?

A.S. [Spells the word.] That means there's a word for the thing on Harry Potter's head!

B. Does that mean there's a name for this? [Touches scar, vaguely villainous, beside his own left eye.]

A.S. [Squints.] What happened?

B. I fell down and I scraped up my face.

A.S. Oh. Well. Yes. [Pause.] Now we can call you "———, yclept 'The Cicatrixed One!'"

[BARISTA stares without a response.]

[Afternoon, patio behind local coffeeshop. A panel of the corrugated metal roof has come unmoored and a wind has curled it back upon itself. A stripe of sunlight rays through the rustic gap, and ANDREW SAULTERS has taken a seat in that light. He is joined on the patio by a MAN WITH CAMERA.]

MAN WITH CAMERA. [Looking upon the patio and seeing no one but ANDREW SAULTERS.] Hello.

ANDREW SAULTERS. Yes. Hello. Am I in your way? I'm about to move.

M.W.C. [Poised between standing straight and retreating.] No.

A.S. Are you sure?

M.W.C. Yes.

A.S. Are you a photographer?

M.W.C. No, I'm a filmmaker.

[A.S. comments on the make and model of his camera.]

M.W.C. Yes, that's it. That's the one. Are you familiar with it?

A.S. No. But I understand it is often used for filmmaking.

M.W.C. It is, yes. [Pause.] How are you today?

[A.S. closes his eyes, shrugs, tilts his head, declines to speak.]

M.W.C. Yes, very good. Entirely convincing.

[Exeunt M.W.C.]

Andrew Saulters and the New Year

[Night, coffeeshop. ANDREW SAULTERS writes queries for a manuscript of poems. He overhears the BARISTA discussing an important matter with her friends.]

BARISTA. I'm excited for what the year brings. I hear that your twenties are for screwing up and your thirties are for getting more into what you learned about yourself.

ANDREW SAULTERS. [Animated by elder wisdom, he raises his hand and calls out]. If I may offer a testimonial from the other side of thirty.

B. [Nods with friendly apprehension.]

A.S. Your twenties are for screwing up, and your thirties are for discovering just how much you screwed up.

[BARISTA gulps, nods, stares.]

Andrew Saulters and the Music of the Spheres

[Interior: coffeeshop at the end of the road, a terribly hot day. ANDREW SAULTERS posts up at the counter to complete press work. A BARISTA addresses to him a query of great importance.]

BARISTA. [Shining a glass with a bar towel.] Hey Andrew. What kind of music do you listen to?

ANDREW SAULTERS. I've been listening to Nick Cave and the Bad Seeds a lot recently. Are you familiar with the Australian rock musician known as Nick Cave?

B. [Squints thoughtfully.] I feel like I've heard of him recently.

A.S. Yeah?

B. [Mystified.] Yeah.

A.S. He's a hard sell.

B. I think someone's mentioned him to me before.

A.S. Here's the deal about Nick Cave and the Bad Seeds. Do you believe in God?

B. Um.

A.S. I understand if this is a personal question.

B. Maybe?

A.S. Very well. I understand. Here's the thing. [Counting off with the fingers of his left hand.] In the songs of Nick Cave and the Bad Seeds, Nick Cave, the songwriter, one, believes in a God, and two, believes that God is evil.

B. [Laughs.] That's a good sell.

A.S. That wasn't even it.

[A.S. describes in detail the various merits and difficulties of the music of Nick Cave and the Bad Seeds, referring in the process to the qualities of no fewer than four albums. B. returns to his actual job. A.S. works on books. Minutes pass in which, unseen and at a great distance, people die without order or explanation, and minute improvements to known inventions are realized but not yet announced. A.S. hails B.]

A.S. I think I know how you heard about Nick Cave and the Bad Seeds.

B. Yeah, somehow someone mentioned them to me recently.

A.S. A few weeks ago. Sitting over there. You asked me what kind of music I listen to. I asked you if you were familiar with the Australian rock musician known as Nick Cave. I did it. It was me.

Andrew Saulters and the Pleasure of the Text

[Slow night in the coffeeshop. ANDREW SAULTERS contemplates book designs while the baristas cast about for things to do. The night wanes. The worn-out decorative lock on SAULTERS' keychain catches the attention of an INQUISITIVE BARISTA.]

ANDREW SAULTERS. I've had that for twenty years. Got it at Aladdin's Arcade way back in the day.

INQUISITIVE BARISTA. [Picks up keys in order to inspect lock.] Does it have, like, space in it? So you can hide a stash in there if you unlock it?

A.S. No, it's just a lock.

COLLEAGUE OF INQUISITIVE BARISTA. Did you ever use it to lock your diary?

A.S. I did not.

C.I.B. I used to have a lock on my diary.

A.S. I keep my diary unsecured. [Pulls diary from bag and drops it on the counter.]

C.I.B. Huh. What do you write in there?

I.B. Do you write about what you do each day? Where you go and what you see and stuff?

A.S. I write about my thoughts.

I.B. Oh, that's scary. You're writing a horror novel, then?

30

Andrew Saulters and the Modern Man

[Morning, coffeeshop.]

BARISTA. Would you like quarters for change, or a fifty-cent piece?
ANDREW SAULTERS. Oh! Fifty-cent piece.

[B. hands A.S. the coin. He examines it.]

A.S. Damn, the guy on here is fine.
B. Huh?
A.S. The fella on here is very attractive.

[He hands the fifty-cent piece to B., who looks at it and hands it back.]

PATRON AT THE END OF BAR. Who's on it?

[A.S. hands the fifty-cent piece to P.A.T.E.O.B. She studies the coin and returns it.]

P.A.T.E.O.B. That's President Kennedy.
A.S. That's a hot dude. I'd do him. I think it's the hair.
FRIEND OF PATRON AT THE END OF BAR. [*Sotto voce.*] It's probably his ass.

Andrew Saulters and the Collective Unconscious

[Afternoon; coffeeshop. ANDREW SAULTERS is settling into his labors after concluding a conversation with a local journalist with whom he had tried to discuss that well-known domestic terrorist, the Unabomber. An ASSOCIATE who had been sitting nearby at the start of the conversation left and has returned.]

ANDREW SAULTERS. Did I scare you away with my talk of the Unabomber?
ASSOCIATE. No.
A.S. I didn't? There was a point where I brought up the Unabomber
 to ————.
A. No, I had to make a phone call.
A.S. You should read the Unabomber's manifesto so you, too, can suddenly and abruptly bring up the Unabomber to strangers one day.

[A beat passes. A.S. wonders whether A. has heard about the Unabomber's manifesto.]

A.S. You don't know about the Unabomber's manifesto.
A. No.
A.S. You don't know about the Unabomber do you.
A. No.
A.S. Get over here and I'll tell you about the Unabomber.

[He describes the Unabomber and his manifesto. Proximate to SAULTERS and his ASSOCIATE, a MAN IN CARGO SHORTS laughs as he fills a cup with water.]

A.S. [To MAN IN CARGO SHORTS]. I'm sorry.

M.C.S. So it's not just me with the religious talk?

A.S. Huh?

M.C.S. There are a bunch of people over there in a really in-depth talk about Jesus.

[M.C.S. turns away, about to depart.]

A.S. You mean you weren't reacting to my talk of the Unabomber.

M.C.S. [Laughing still.] No, who's the Unabomber?

Andrew Saulters and the Space Between Spaces

[Middle of a long afternoon. Downtown coffeeshop in which the sun has bleached everything beyond perception, into bright planes. The air does not stir. ANDREW SAULTERS perches at the bar and reflects the stillness of the scene back at itself. He considers his next sentence. The BARISTA chances to look upon him.]

BARISTA. Oh, sorry—do you need something?

ANDREW SAULTERS. No. I'm looking for insight.

B. Oh, you mean the flies?

A.S. No.

B. I thought you said "insects."

A.S. No.

Andrew Saulters and the Empty Space

[Coffeeshop. He is typing an email to students when he is hailed by a FAMILIAR REGULAR PATRON. The PATRON scans the list of student names next to SAULTERS' computer, reading the first.]

FAMILIAR REGULAR PATRON. "A————."

ANDREW SAULTERS. "V————." "K————." "A———— F————."
    "V———— J————."

FRP. [Studying the end of the list, which has an empty space with no name.] Then there's an empty space.

A.S. Yes.

F.R.P. With no name.

A.S. Yes.

F.R.P. If you're a Zen practitioner, the empty space is the most important part.

A.S. Are you a Zen practitioner, S———— M————?

F.R.P. No.

A.S. How do you know that?

F.R.P. I don't know.

A.S. How do you know which question I was asking?

F.R.P. Whoa.

Andrew Saulters and the End of Innocence

[Evening, coffeeshop. ANDREW SAULTERS piles upon his table his bookmaking instruments in preparation for an interval of labor. He is hailed by an OUTGOING YOUTH who has unpacked a deck of cards at his own table.]

OUTGOING YOUTH. [Over shoulder, leaning back in his chair and without any prior utterance.] *HEY!*

[ANDREW SAULTERS crumples his brow and narrows his eyes into an expression of confusion, hoping to signify disdain at having been hailed in such a way.]

O.Y. [Registering no offense.] Do you remember how to play "Go Fish?"
A.S. No.

Andrew Saulters and the Men Who Won the War

[Twilight in the big city. Slight rain. ANDREW SAULTERS slouches at the counter of a coffeeshop he used to frequent when he lived up the street many years ago. His attempt to identify a particular posterweight sans serif font has failed, and after staring at the computer screen for hours he has begun to wonder whether it is the search for the font or the idea of the font itself that is more fruitless. Did I really see one like the one I thought I saw, he is thinking. He heaves an audible sigh and sets his eyes toward the horizon. A MAN IN A BACKWARDS BALL CAP, also sitting at the counter, addresses him.]

MAN IN A BACKWARDS BALL CAP. Giving up for the night?

ANDREW SAULTERS. Yes. It is time to do the real work.

M.B.B.C. Oh? What is the real work?

A.S. I'm in town for a couple of weeks to teach creative writing. I've never taught a course like this before. I have a lot of preparation to do.

M.B.B.C. Ah.

A.S. And what do you do?

M.B.B.C. Oh, I do a few things. I trade stocks. Sell guns.

Andrew Saulters and Adulthood in America

[Dusk, food truck. A BALL-CAPPED SMOKER studies the chalk menu mounted on the mobile kitchen. ANDREW SAULTERS asks the SMOKER if he is in line, and he says he is not, pleading difficulty reading the menu due to a series of strokes. A conversation develops, in which the SMOKER launches a broadside against the American dream.]

BALL-CAPPED SMOKER. [Waving hand with cigarette.] There's this expectation, you know, that if you just have this nice job, you can have this nice apartment, this nice car, this nice life, if you just work hard. But most of the time you're just fed up with the job!

ANDREW SAULTERS. [Hands in pockets, waiting.] For sure. What did you used to do?

B.C.S. I was a nurse. Giving back was my thing, because before then I had done a lot of taking. A lot of taking!

A.S. Oh?

B.C.S. You know, if you think your life is shit, if you're miserable now, you should just wait, because everything can change in a second.

A.S. That ain't wrong!

B.C.S. So what do you do?

A.S. [Actually thinking.] I freelance a lot of things.

B.C.S. [Draws a breath through cigarette.] You know, the way you say that, you could be anything from a hitman to an IT guy.

A.S. Yeah.

B.C.S. The way you say "Yeah," I'm guessing hitman.

A.S. [In head.] What am I?

The Night is Dark, Andrew Saulters, and You Are Far from Home

[Sidwalk; a cold night. ANDREW SAULTERS walks home with his bicycle, considering various ideas pertaining to desert. For instance: "It seems impossible that anyone generally *deserves* the caring attention of anyone else, yet it seems irresponsible to decline the commitment to care for other people generally. It could be desert is not the premise upon which to establish an ethic of mutual care." He walks. The night is dark and he does not look at the stars. A motorist pulls up beside him—it is the LAST PATRON OF THE COFFEESHOP where ten minutes ago SAULTERS was the next-to-last patron.]

LAST PATRON OF THE COFFEESHOP. [Through passenger window.]
    You haven't made it very far!
ANDREW SAULTERS. It's hard not to read that as a metaphor!

Andrew Saulters and Frames of War

[Interior: downtown bar at night. The baseball game goes to rain delay and the YANKEES FAN next to ANDREW SAULTERS asks him what he is reading.]

A.S. Some poems by Zbigniew Herbert.

Y.F. Where's he from?

A.S. Poland, I think.

Y.F. Ah. When did he write?

A.S. 1958 to 1998. At least that's what the spine says.

Y.F. What's he write about?

A.S. Lots of political stuff. It's amazing to read political poetry that doesn't suck. It's something American poets can't do, you know? It's like it's not available to us. Perhaps if we saw more oppression or experienced more death firsthand....

Y.F. Yeah, maybe if a soldier wrote some poetry—

A.S. No, that too is disappointing. There's something about who we are that keeps us from being able to do it. It's not available to us.

Y.F. Yeah, you've got to be able to see it firsthand—

A.S. No, actually, I don't think that's it. We've got firsthand experience now. The experience of supporting a globally-deployed army with its boot in the back of anyone who resists American hegemony is this experience. That experience is this one, right here.

Y.F. You've got to see it firsthand, yeah.

40

Andrew Saulters and a Conversation over Drinks

New York Pizza, summer. While reading Richard Hendel's *On Book Design*, ANDREW SAULTERS is interrupted by a STRANGER in his middle fifties who sits in his booth and attempts to make small talk about his, SAULTERS', life. SAULTERS wonders if this is his, the STRANGER's, method of procuring one night stands, or might his behavior be a mere artifact of prolonged loneliness? SAULTERS dismisses him shortly. Months later, the STRANGER will resurface to ask drunkenly, "Excuse me, do you know the Hebrew or Jewish word I am thinking of?" When SAULTERS fails to determine the word, he says so, and the STRANGER totters away to the depths of the bar from which he came.

Mellow Mushroom, summer. ANDREW SAULTERS is reading *The Dream Songs* when an ADORABLE COUPLE in their fifties invites him to discourse upon multiple topics, including but not limited to the delightful mechanical characteristics of the Volkswagen Type 1 engine. SAULTERS wonders if, really, they are travelling serial killers, or else cult leaders.

New York Pizza, winter. Writing in his journal, ANDREW SAULTERS is prodded by a RAIN-COATED MAN seated beside the television: "Hey, is that your journal you're writing? Is that in English? You've got, like, nice handwriting." SAULTERS thanks him and hies out the door for a long walk through snow.

Mellow Mushroom, fall. ANDREW SAULTERS is reading Ed Sanders' *Investigative Poetry* when the ADORABLE COUPLE from two years before hails him from down the bar. "Hello again! How are you?" the man asks, having greeted him by name. "You must be a regular here," the woman says. SAULTERS squints, admits that he can sometimes be found there.

New York Pizza, summer. ANDREW SAULTERS is editing a manuscript of poetry when a RECENTLY DISCHARGED MARINE inquires of him, "Hey. What are you doing?" Also: "Why don't you stop?"

College Hill, fall. Ensconced by manuscripts in his booth, ANDREW SAULTERS is reading submissions to the press when a QUIET MAN approaches and asks, "What are you doing?" SAULTERS says he is reading. "Yes, but what are you doing?" SAULTERS says he is reading. "Thanks for your time."

Mellow Mushroom, fall. While attempting to write about the suicide of a stranger known to him, ANDREW SAULTERS gains the notice of a MOTHER-DAUGHTER duo beginning the second drink. "Is that your journal?" "Are you studying?" "Is that English?" "Why do you write like that?" His brief answers fail to stanch their curiosities. Thereafter the pair deliver a disquisition in which mental health diagnoses, philandering husbands, the general decline of the American male since 1960, a wayward son-in-law, the resemblance of SAULTERS to that same wayward son-in-law, a wayward son, the scheming deadbeat girlfriends of that same wayward son, and the need to write a mother-daughter memoir are discoursed upon, proclaimed, or else announced. SAULTERS smiles and nods throughout, silently reproaching himself for the record of prodigious verbal performance that has apparently necessitated such protracted karmic retribution. He finishes his drink and gathers his writerly equipage. "Do you know another bar like this in town?" the MOTHER asks. Offering the name of a place he never goes and wishing a good evening, SAULTERS exits into the mist and tumult of an approaching hurricane.

College Hill, summer. ANDREW SAULTERS has arrived to do some journaling. He runs into a TALKATIVE YOUTH with whom he has had some stimulating discussions on prior occasions. What is Andrew Saulters doing, asks the YOUTH. SAULTERS reports on his intentions and thereafter is derailed into conversation that does not last long—the YOUTH discloses he has suffered some verbal indignity out on the patio and now he must fight the villain. Do not fight him, urges SAULTERS, but vengeance by fisticuffs cannot be averted. The affronted YOUTH manfully challenges his opponent and soon they are in the street, a pitiful spectacle, a fuss of missed swings and loose clutches at shirtsleeves. The brawl finishes, and collectively the onlookers experience disappointment in the familiar shabbiness of such affairs. Many drinks are ordered. As police sirens sound in the distance, SAULTERS recommends to the YOUTH that he run for it, but his brash associate will not leave the scene without being led by the elbow, so intent is he on stating his cause before the law. SAULTERS walks some distance to deposit him in his, the YOUTH's, rented rooms and returns to the bar to pay his, SAULTERS', tab. Regarding SAULTERS as the YOUTH's mild chaperone, the bartenders report that he has stiffed them for the tip.

Andrew Saulters and the Seven Seas

[Early morning, Winston-Salem. Attired in browning hat, &c., ANDREW SAULTERS passes down the central avenue, observing the city's awakening. A FELLOW RECLINING UPON A SIDEWALK BENCH hails him gaily.]

FELLOW RECLINING UPON A SIDEWALK BENCH. [Laughing, gesturing.] Hey, man! You look like Captain Jack!

ANDREW SAULTERS. [Uncertain, walking on.] Is that so? I don't even know who that is!

F.R.U.S.B. [Laughing, waving.] It's a drink, man!

Andrew Saulters and the Best Lawyer in Town

[It's a cold, rainy, windy day in the city. ANDREW SAULTERS in greatcoat and hat, the works of Adrienne Rich and Caesar Vallejo tucked to his chest, makes slight progress through the turbulence. A STRANGER WITH POCKETED HANDS, hunched to preserve warmth, approaches from the opposite direction. It appears the STRANGER will pass without communication, but at the last moment, he looks SAULTERS in the eye and speaks.]

STRANGER WITH POCKETED HANDS. Hey man, I hear you're the best lawyer in town!

[Exeunt STRANGER WITH POCKETED HANDS.]

Andrew Saulters and the First Cut

[Evening, downtown. ANDREW SAULTERS hunches into the cold winds of March. He is underway to the corner store for adhesive bandages, a measure to protect his finger calluses while he binds books. A STRANGER ten yards distant sees SAULTERS, hails him.]

STRANGER. Hey! You remember me?
ANDREW SAULTERS. No.

[Cry of wind curling around the sharp corners of buildings. The STRANGER and SAULTERS pass each other soundlessly.]

Andrew Saulters and a Moment of True Feeling

[Parking lot, hot afternoon. ANDREW SAULTERS carries his equipage to a not-very-pressing engagement. A MAN whom he has seen often in the parking lot calls out to him.]

PARKING LOT MAN. Hey, can I show you something?

ANDREW SAULTERS. No. I'm sorry.

P.L.M. Why are you apologizing?

A.S. I'm sorry, I have a pressing meeting.

P.L.M. But why are you apologizing?

A.S. I can't see what you're asking me to look at.

P.L.M. Why apologize though?

A.S. I'm being polite.

Andrew Saulters et la Système de la Mode

[Grey afternoon, parking lot. ANDREW SAULTERS has just walked from his parked vehicle to his home and back, a distance of a few miles. He had locked his keys in the truck. Lightly attired all in brown, he finds the cold, foggy air delightful to breathe and walk in. When he closes in on the truck, BOY ON A BICYCLE rolls toward him, a couple of dollar bills clenched in his left hand. The youngster makes polite conversation.]

BOY ON BICYCLE. Hey! What are you dressed as?

ANDREW SAULTERS. Myself. This is how I dress.

B.O.B. Oh, all right. I like your hat.

A.S. Thanks. It used to be black. [Shows bottom of hat brim.] Now it's brown. [Points to exterior of hat.]

B.O.B. You spray-painted it?

A.S. No, I've had it for 12 years. It changed color in the sun.

B.O.B. Sweet. How long have you had that shirt?

A.S. This is a light coat, not a shirt. Six months, I guess.

B.O.B. Okay, thanks!

[BOY ON BICYCLE pedals away.]

48

Andrew Saulters and the Finale of Seem

[Night in Tampa. Pharmacy with blinding interior lights. ANDREW SAULTERS approaches the CASHIER. He hasn't slept for 36 hours. His truck died in rural Florida and he abandoned it there. He is questioning decisions that go back months and years, but they can't be taken back anyway. His reflection in store windows reminds him of the startled asymmetry of Ralph Nader's face after the onset of Bell's Palsy. The CASHIER is an older woman with a bright smile and red glasses frames. He is buying twelve ounces of apple juice.]

CASHIER. $2.67. [Looking SAULTERS over]. My, you're stylish!
ANDREW SAULTERS. Oh. Thanks.

[SAULTERS has located two dollar bills, and he searches his pockets for a third. He knows that somewhere he has a third dollar bill. The CASHIER waits. The customers behind SAULTERS wait. SAULTERS, too, waits.]

Andrew Saulters and a Discourse on Inequality

[Bookfair, conference center. Writers circulate among publishers' tables. The hour, fluorescently illuminated, is unknowable, and shall not be known. ANDREW SAULTERS captains a table representing a small press and reads the final chapter in a book on debt. Across the aisle from him, four children orbit a table run by their mother. A GIRL WITH A LOLLIPOP approaches him.]

GIRL WITH A LOLLIPOP. Hi. [Steps quietly behind table.]

ANDREW SAULTERS. [Seated and shifting away slightly.] Hello. Yes?

G.W.L. [Licks lollipop, wiggles, stares vacantly.] Do you have any candy?

A.S. No, I don't have any candy.

G.W.L. I have more candy than you.

A.S. Yes. You do have more candy than me.

[Exeunt GIRL WITH LOLLIPOP.]

Andrew Saulters and the Inductive Mode

[Hot afternoon, resplendent college campus. ANDREW SAULTERS chaperones his students during their fifteen-minute break. He takes a long draught of water from the glass bottle his students have been misidentifying all week as a flask. A student addresses him matter-of-factly as she hula-hoops.]

STUDENT. Mr. Saulters?

ANDREW SAULTERS. Yes, A————?

S. I think you're a hipster.

A.S. Is that so?

S. Yes.

A.S. Well, come on then. What's your argument?

S. You wear a hat.

A.S. [Self-conscious, he adjusts the hat against the sun.] True.

S. And you drink water out of a glass bottle.

A.S. Yes?

S. And you have a beard.

A.S. Indeed.

S. You wear glasses.

A.S. [Throws hands in air.] As if since birth! But none of that makes one a hipster, no?

S. You manage an indie publishing company.

A.S. Huh.

Andrew Saulters and the Wages of Fame

[Busy afternoon, college coffeeshop. ANDREW SAULTERS is scribbling in his notebook about "Inside Llewyn Davis," a film that has confused him despite repeat viewings. Could the problem be, SAULTERS wonders, that he identifies more with the brittle minor gatekeepers at the fringes of the scene than with the musicians? That, for instance, he sees less of himself in Davis than Mel Novikoff, the elderly owner of the tiny label that has signed Davis? He is considering the question in meandering prose when an ENTHUSIASTIC COMMENTATOR interrupts him with an important brief.]

ENTHUSIASTIC COMMENTATOR. You were in the newspaper!
ANDREW SAULTERS. [He stops writing but remains hunched forward with pen in hand.] I'm sorry?
E.C. You were in the newspaper!
A.S. Yes. Who are you?
E.C. [No longer visibly enthusiastic.] I saw you in the newspaper.
A.S. Sure, but what's your name? That's, like, a real question.

[E.C. says his first name. It is one syllable that he pronounces with a rising intonation.]

A.S. Okay, and what's your last name?

[E.C. says his last name: two syllables, pronounced as a question.]

A.S. [Extends his hand.] It's nice to meet you, ——— ———.

[Exeunt E.C., face imprinted with discomfort.]

Andrew Saulters and His Magnificent Ukulele

[Greyhound bus, early morning. ANDREW SAULTERS, accoutred in tweed jacket and felted wool hat, is seated at the back of the bus beside a RETURNING TRAVELER who has been on the road for twenty-two hours and will continue for fourteen more. SAULTERS has slept one hour within the last twenty-four. The fatigue of both passengers is evident in their eyes, their poor postures. All around, parents are sleeping with infant children. The day is overcast and will remain so. The TRAVELLER amiably discourses upon an undifferentiated series of topics and SAULTERS attempts to respond with good humor.]

RETURNING TRAVELLER. [Rummages through his backpack.] So, you like pot?

ANDREW SAULTERS. [Gazing out window at features of the passing landscape.] Sorry?

R.T. Like, marijuana?

A.S. [Squints slightly, indicates the negative by shaking his head.]

R.T. Do you like drugs?

A.S. They do not have much appeal to me? I have always had other things to do instead.

R.T. [Zips the backpack.] Yeah, I hear that. Sometimes I think the people I've seen lose it with drugs were just bored. Anyway, you just looked like the kind of guy who seemed like he would like them.

[A.S. turns to the window. Leaning against the glass, he hopes to sleep.]

R.T. [Gazing at his smart telephone] Hey. You know, you look like...

A.S. [Turns to R.T. and nods twice, waiting for completion of the simile.]

R.T. ...like...like, he's a musician...

A.S. Oh, which one?

R.T. He was in a band.

A.S. Whom did he play with?

R.T. He was in The Beatles...

A.S. You mean John Lennon.

R.T. Yeah! John Lennon. You look like him.

A.S. I have gotten that before. I have also been likened to Felix Cavaliere, though I do not see it.

R.T. You just look like him.

[A.S. nods to indicate an understanding of the description. He turns to the window and stares blankly at the countryside. R.T. attempts to baby talk with an infant across the aisle, but he is discouraged by the mother. He disengages.]

R.T. [Gazing up the aisle, through the windshield of the bus, which is very far away.] Say, you Amish?

Andrew Saulters and the Identities

[Dusk. Having just boarded the train, ANDREW SAULTERS is settling in for a lengthy ride. An EXCITABLE PASSENGER on the way to his seat seizes upon him in recognition.]

EXCITABLE PASSENGER. Hey! I know you!

ANDREW SAULTERS. [Quietly awaits the details of this recognition.]

E.P. I must have met you in, like, Chattanooga, or New York.

A.S. [Does not recognize E.P.] I'm sorry, but are you sure?

E.P. Yeah, I know you! I'm W———— C————! I've seen you before! In Chattanooga, or—

A.S. Do you remember my name?

E.P. No, sorry, man. Or maybe it was Greensboro?

A.S. I have been mistaken for 39 people in the last 15 years. Let me show you the list—

E.P. No, man, it was Greensboro!

[A.S. hands E.P. the list. E.P. looks at it quickly and returns it.]

E.P. You know M———— S————?

A.S. Yes—he was on that list—

E.P. Yeah, I play with M———— S———— all the time. At NYP! Obviously you're not him.

A.S. [Still does not recognize E.P.] Yeah.

E.P. So I know you from Greensboro! What's your name, man? You're not super-secretive, are you?

A.S. [Pause.] No. [He gives his name.]

Andrew Saulters and the Deductive Mode

[Greensboro; dining quarters of the health & wellness supermarket. Surrounded by notes and open books, ANDREW SAULTERS hunches over a large black journal, writing in quarter-inch block script. A MAN with a large beard and great round eyes approaches him, clutching a jar of green olives. Of tremendous stature, he bends toward SAULTERS as he addresses him.]

MAN WITH JAR OF OLIVES. I just have to ask you: What are you working on?

ANDREW SAULTERS. It is my journal.

M.J.O. Daily?

A.S. [Equivocating gesture.] Eh.

M.J.O. Are you from here?

A.S. No.

M.J.O. Are you foreign?

A.S. No.

M.J.O. Just moving around?

A.S. I'm from Alabama.

M.J.O. So you're a student, then?

A.S. No.

M.J.O. Oh.

[Exeunt M.J.O.]

Andrew Saulters and the Outsider at the Heart of Things

[Cool night on the patio of the local bar, where a large crowd mills about, smoking and carousing. As ANDREW SAULTERS, attired in long coat and hat, makes passage among the merrymakers, a SERIOUS YOUNG MAN beckons him.]

SERIOUS YOUNG MAN. [Smoking.] Hey, how you doing. What's your name?

ANDREW SAULTERS. [Half-turned in preparation for departure, he identifies himself.] I'm well. And what is your name?

S.Y.M. [Hand extended for greeting.] I'm R———. Say, you a student?

A.S. [Greets him.] No.

S.Y.M. [Smoking, looking about.] You live around here?

A.S. [Pauses.] Sort of.

S.Y.M. You got anything in that coat I got to worry about?

A.S. I'm not sure what you mean by that.

S.Y.M. That's a big coat. I'm worried you got something in there I got to worry about.

A.S. You worry about a lot of stuff, R———.

S.Y.M. It's something I do. I see someone wearing a big coat and I need to know, do you have anything in there I need to worry about?

A.S. Just my body.

S.Y.M. I hope to see it sometime.

Andrew Saulters and the Last Word

[A cool Sunday afternoon in downtown Chattanooga. ANDREW SAULTERS ambles without imperative when he is hailed by a WOMAN SITTING ON A HALF-WALL.]

WOMAN SITTING ON HALF-WALL. Hey! Buy me lunch!
ANDREW SAULTERS. [Stops.] I'm sorry, I don't have any money on me.
W.S.H.W. Uh huh.

[A.S. walks on.]

W.S.H.W. Hey! Where your wife at?
A.S. I am unmarried.
W.S.H.W. [Looking away.] Ah.

Andrew Saulters and the Decrepit Torso of Apollo

[The sun has appeared for the first time in a week. ANDREW SAULTERS waits for a teller at the neighborhood bank. Service is slow. After a few minutes, a CHATTY CUSTOMER joins the line.]

CHATTY CUSTOMER. [Pointing to a teller who is working on a task without taking anyone from the line]. Is she open?
ANDREW SAULTERS. [Turning about.] I'm sorry?
C.C. Is that teller open?
A.S. No. She is engaged on another matter.
C.C. Oh.

[Time passes.]

C.C. Why, you sure do have a lot of hair!
A.S. Excuse me?
C.C. You've got hair all over your body!
A.S. Yes. It's all over.
C.C. Why, even on your chest...
A.S. Yes, I do. It's how I came out, I guess.
C.C. I bet you have hair like that everywhere...like even on your back?
A.S. Well, sure. I wouldn't know, really.

[C.C.'s animated face freezes, demonstrating her confusion.]

A.S. Being that it's my back.
C.C. You must not have a mirror in your shower like I do.
A.S. No. No, I do not.

Andrew Saulters: Dasein, Sein und Zeit

[Night, bar. For ANDREW SAULTERS, glasses off, the world is mostly a blur. He is passing among the books he has stacked before himself on the counter. He reads the passage in Safranski's Heidegger biography that discusses his aversion to superficial personalities of the type to be found among coffeeshop intellectuals discussing Nietzsche and points out that Heidegger himself was often confused for the school janitor. The other four patrons are watching a football game on mute. The bar is very quiet when a PATRON makes an extravagant exit.]

EXITING PATRON. *ROLL TIDE!* [He departs.]

ANDREW SAULTERS. [To the blank space before him, the air.] I am from Alabama. I cannot stand that team.

[The PATRON NEXT TO SAULTERS turns partially toward him. The BARTENDER looks at him. The bar is silent.]

A.S. They're, uh, they're playing right now aren't they?

PATRON SITTING NEXT TO SAULTERS. [Watching game.] Yes.

PATRON AT OTHER END OF THE BAR. Can we get some volume up there? It's real quiet in here. Like a library in here.

BARTENDER. Sure thing.

Andrew Saulters and the Anxiety of Influence

[Pizza parlor; slow night. ANDREW SAULTERS reads Caesar Vallejo aloud in a low voice while he waits for the MAN BEHIND THE COUNTER to prepare his pizza. They are alone in the room.]

ANDREW SAULTERS. "I have a terrible fear that I may be an animal / of white snow, who has kept his father and mother / alive with his solitary circulation through the veins, / and a fear that on this day which is so marvellous, sunny, archbishoprical, / (a day that stands so for night) / this animal, like a straight line, / will manage not to be happy, or to breathe, / or to turn into something else—"

MAN BEHIND THE COUNTER. [Kneading dough.] Are you married?

A.S. No. Are you?

M.B.C. Trying to be! [Rolling dough.] I think I will be one day.

A.S. I'm not thinking I will be.

M.B.C. Why?

A.S. Many reasons.

M.B.C. [Flattening dough across pan.] You like to be alone?

A.S. That is one reason.

M.B.C. All the girls who work here talk about you. That is, they have as long as I've worked here.

A.S. I'm easier to talk about than to talk to.

[M.B.C. shrugs and heads to the oven.]

A.S. [Resumes.] "Oh to roll on the ground, to be there, to cough, to wrap oneself, / to wrap the doctrine, the temple, from shoulder to shoulder, / to go away, to cry, to let it go for eight / or for seven or for six, for five, or let it go / for life with its three possibilities!" [In head.] "It." "It." What is the "it" he would like to let go?

Andrew Saulters and the Pep Talk

[College student union; afternoon. ANDREW SAULTERS attempts to encourage a STUDENT whose desire to produce nothing but the best work has kept her from starting the most recent assignment, about which she has several doubts. He enters the big finish.]

ANDREW SAULTERS. Wanting so much from your work on the first draft can keep you from trying at all; you discourage yourself before you even begin. I'm talking from experience here. Would you believe that I was at one time and sometimes still am a perfectionist?

STUDENT. [Pause.] No. [Pause.] No, I would not.

Andrew Saulters and the Masque of Authority

[Classroom: mid-morning, fluorescent lights. ANDREW SAULTERS is inscrutably holding forth about images and exposition. His writing students struggle valiantly past the indignity of the tutelage, their faces blank with exhaustion or else marked with ineffable grief. He prepares to introduce the modes of rhetoric.]

ANDREW SAULTERS. I think we should talk about the modes of rhetoric. [Pauses. Inclining his head, he recalls a pleasant memory.] Huh—I think we could get an echo in here if we try. [Singing it out in a rising tone, with tremendous volume toward the end.] It's time for us to speak about: [He moves his hands across his plane of vision like he can see the words as he proclaims them.] *THE MODES OF RHETORIC!*

[The words echo and the students snap to face him. A—— raises her hand.]

A.S. Yes, A——?
A——. That was loud!
A.S. Oh, I'm sorry about that. I didn't mean to alarm anyone.

[T—— raises her hand.]

A.S. Yes, T——?
T——. You should talk like that all the time!
A.S. But—but I was very loud just then. That was difficult for me.

[S—— raises her hand.]

A.S. Yes, s————.

s————. Yeah, but it's hard to hear you sometimes? Your voice is very low.

A.S. Yes, that's true. And how I struggle with it! I hereby pledge to work on the volume of my voice along with the rest of my elocution. So, has anyone heard about the modes of rhetoric?

[c———— raises her hand.]

A.S. Yes, c————.

c————. I mean, that was loud, but it wasn't that loud.

A.S. You think so? That was...that was...tremendously loud, don't you think? I mean, I couldn't do that for six hours a day. [Touches hand to chest.] My heart!

[A———— raises her hand.]

A.S. Yes, A————.

A————. [With excitement and some nostalgia.] That's nothing like what my English teacher did—you could hear him down the hall! When I had a class above his room, you could hear him through the floor!

A.S. And you liked that?

A————. Well, it did keep you awake.

A.S. Ah, yes. "Kept us awake"—reminds me of the FBI at Waco!

[N———— raises her hand.]

A.S. Yes, N———.

N———. You could do every other word loud, so then you would save your voice!

A.S. i COULD do EVERY other WORD like THAT? that's ALMOST more DIFFICULT!

[s——— raises her hand.]

A.S. Yes, s———.

s———. I had a history teacher who was really into World War II, and he was a great teacher and everything, but sometimes it was hard to pay attention when he went over all the battles because he had this monotone, so he would say stuff like, "And here's what happened at this battle. And here's what happened at this one. And now I am taking my shirt off." And no one noticed!

A.S. I see?

[T——— raises her hand.]

A.S. Yes, T———.

T———. I had a teacher once who would say stuff like "Now make that a *sassy* comma," just to see if we were paying attention.

A.S. That—that's terrifying.

[s——— raises her hand.]

A.S. Yes, s———.

s———. We need you to shout to keep us paying attention.

A.S. I believe I've heard certain totalitarian governments make the same argument, no?

[Students laugh.]

A.S. [Gesturing for quiet.] So, has anyone heard of the modes of rhetoric? [Pauses.] Anyone?

[Pause.]

Andrew Saulters and the Mark of Assurance

[Daylight bright classroom. ANDREW SAULTERS prepares for lecture a few minutes before class. His right hand and arm bear scabbed-over road rashes from a bicycle crash earlier in the week, and he has not commented on them to his students. He feels worn out for no reason he knows, and a STUDENT observes his apparent fatigue.]

STUDENT 1. You seem tired.

ANDREW SAULTERS. Indeed I am.

STUDENT 2. What happened to your arm?

A.S. [Gestures to abrasions.] You mean here?

STUDENT 2. Yeah. What is that?

STUDENT 3. Is that from, like, a bike crash?

A.S. [Without looking up from computer.] Leprosy.

[Students fall silent.]

A.S. No, I'm just kidding! It's really from a bike crash!

[Students remain silent.]

A.S. I mean, it's not a very funny joke. But it's a joke.

Andrew Saulters and the End of the Semester

[Classroom; clear morning. It is the final day of the semester, when students are offered the class period to work on the portfolio, which is their last assignment. ANDREW SAULTERS no longer has a voice, and whenever he speaks he can manage only a hoarse whisper, conspicuous as Jake Gittes' face wound in "Chinatown." To soothe the classroom's silence, he has put on Philip Glass' "Koyaanisqatsi" soundtrack. Students have slowly slipped away as the class continues, until one STUDENT remains.]

ANDREW SAULTERS. Music's a hard sell, no?

STUDENT. It is...dull for a Friday morning.

A.S. It doesn't have words!

[Student makes confused expression.]

A.S. When you're writing, it's hard to listen to music with words, right?

S. I listen to music with words when I write all the time.

A.S. Ah.

S. What music, with words, do you listen to when you write?

A.S. [Turns to face computer.] Bob Dylan. Have you heard his most recent album?

S. No.

A.S. It has a fourteen-minute-long song about the sinking of the *Titanic*. [Excited by the thought.] That's just long enough to close out the semester!

[A.S starts "Tempest," the second-to-last song on the album of the same name.]

69

VOICE OF BOB DYLAN. [In rolling ballad measure.] "The pale moon rose in its glory, out on the western town. She told a sad, sad story of the great ship that went down..."

s. [Gets up to look at the screen.] This really goes on for fourteen minutes, doesn't it?

A.S. [Nods.]

v.o.b.d. "...The watchman, he lay dreaming, as the ballroom dancers twirled. He dreamed the *Titanic* was sinking into the underworld..."

s. [Scrutinizes album cover, points to release date.] Wait! You said this was his most recent album.

A.S. It is.

s. This says it's from 2012!

A.S. It is.

v.o.b.d. "...Lights were holding steady, gliding over the foam. All the lords and ladies heading for their eternal home..."

Andrew Saulters and the Sacred and the Profane

[Cloudy evening. Modish bar, half-full. Sitting alone at a long table that could accommodate as many as eight patrons, ANDREW SAULTERS is composing a letter of interest for a job. There's a woman reading Questlove at the counter, a few men on smart telephones, a birthday party for two identically-dressed six-year-olds. Millennials, he says to himself. There's an old fellow, a restless berg of a man, wearing a button-down shirt with no sleeves, who alleges his beer is made of pine needles. The MAN WITHOUT SLEEVES begins to pace the floor of the bar, speaking incoherently. He stops, addressing SAULTERS directly.]

MAN WITHOUT SLEEVES. [Pointing with left hand, holding last fifth of a pint of gose in right.] YOU. YOU LOVE JESUS.
ANDREW SAULTERS. [Unsure how to understand him.] I'm sorry?
M.W.S. AH! [He turns about.]

[A.S. looks around to see if anyone else is registering this interaction. No one is registering this interaction. It is as if A.S. and M.W.S. have become unpeople. A.S. smiles at M.W.S. on purpose.]

M.W.S. I'll teach you! [He paces, swings about, speaks incoherently. Looks directly at A.S. from a couple of steps off.] I TAUGHT YOU!

[A.S. closes computer and continues smiling, asking himself if M.W.S. resembles any of his previous teachers.]

M.W.S. I SETTLED! [Paces back to the bar, finishes his pint, places the glass deliberately on the counter. He points at A.S.] YOU SETTLED! [M.W.S. exits bar defiantly.]
A.S. [Looking down at the table, to himself.] Yes. I settled.

Andrew Saulters : Surveiller et Punir

[Night. ANDREW SAULTERS stops at a red traffic signal in a quiet restaurant district. In a parking lot to his left, a car has been parked with its headlights on. For the brightness of the lights, nothing beyond the car is visible. An UNSEEN MAN calls out SAULTERS' name.]

ANDREW SAULTERS. [Squinting, he searches the darkness for the one who has hailed him.] Who are you? [He grabs a flashlight from the glove compartment and shines it into the night.]

UNSEEN MAN. [Waves with right hand.] It's B——— from the Green Bean!

A.S. [Locates U.M.'s face with light. U.M. squints in discomfort.] Ah, so it is. It's very hard for me to see when I have a light in my eyes. [A.S. locates a second man beside the car with the flashlight.]

U.M. [Still waving with right hand when A.S. fixes him with flashlight again.] It's like I'm being detained!

A.S. You are, in a manner of speaking.

[The traffic signal turns green. SAULTERS departs.]

Andrew Saulters and the Heat of the Night

[A muggy night. ANDREW SAULTERS walks back from the corner store at a heightened pace. From the dark window of his cruiser, a POLICE OFFICER hails him.]

POLICE OFFICER. [Fixing his flashlight on SAULTERS.] Hey. What do you have in your hand?

ANDREW SAULTERS. [Raises his right hand, in which he holds a canned beverage.]

P.O. Yeah, what is that?

A.S. It is a Starbucks-brand vanilla-flavored espresso beverage.

[Exeunt OFFICER in cruiser. A.S. flips him the bird. Two students address A.S. from their porch, having witnessed the back and forth.]

WOMAN ON PORCH. Did that just happen?

A.S. Yeah, he didn't even ask about what I have in my back pocket. [Removes from his back pocket a glass bottle of water that resembles a flask of vodka.]

MAN ON PORCH. Man! And I just lit up a bowl over here!

Andrew Saulters and the Necessities

[Midnight at the corner store. Nothing has gone wrong, nothing has gone right. ANDREW SAULTERS approaches the counter and hands the CASHIER his purchases: a bag of potato chips and a stick of butter.]

ANDREW SAULTERS. [Grandly raising his voice]. Ah yes! A man needs no more than a bag of chips and a stick of butter!

CASHIER. [Ringing up the items.] Yes. Is that all?

A.S. Perhaps a man also needs the guidance of some deity or cause greater than himself, although who am I to say?

C. I'm sorry?

A.S. Oh, nothing.

C. $3.44.

A.S. Of course.

74

Comeuppance is Nigh, Andrew Saulters

[Afternoon, coffeeshop. ANDREW SAULTERS wheezes under the influence of certain allergies. He sights a FAMILIAR PERSON and makes eye contact in preparation to hail him. SAULTERS approaches.]

FAMILIAR PERSON. [Apprehends the relentless eye contact of SAULTERS, who has said nothing]. Hi.

ANDREW SAULTERS. W———!

[F.P. is silent.]

A.S. [Recognition of his error dawns upon him.] Oh no! You're not W———!

F.P. No.

A.S. I'm so sorry!

F.P. It's okay—

A.S. You don't understand! I've been mistaken for 49 people over the last 17 years, and I hate it every time, and I've just duplicated the experience for you!

F.P. No, it's okay.

A.S. It isn't! I saw you in the bookstore yesterday, and I said, "Hello, W———," and you didn't respond.

F.P. I must not have heard you.

A.S. Probably not. I was at your 4:00. [He indicates where 4:00 would be for F.P. at the present moment.]

F.P. W——— is my roommate.

A.S. Oh, so you know each other?

F.P. Yes. He is my roommate.

A.S. You mean to say you're related?

F.P. No. We just look alike. Similar hair, same look.

A.S. That's certainly true.

F.P. Yes.

A.S. I'm very sorry.

Andrew Saulters and the Theory of Forms

[Coffeeshop, midday. Quiet, listless. ANDREW SAULTERS performs his daily labor as the baristas talk between themselves. He glancingly overhears a remark.]

BARISTA. I just can't deal with everybody. Unless everyone were Andrew Saulters.

ANDREW SAULTERS. [With uncertainty, he looks up to face the invoker of his name.] That shouldn't be. No one should be Andrew Saulters.

Andrew Saulters and the Tunnel at the End of the Light

[Afternoon, coffeeshop. ANDREW SAULTERS struggles under the weight of his considerable equipage. The BARISTA stops sweeping and remarks that he is in earlier than usual. Why is that, he wants to know. They banter, but never is it developed why he has deviated from routine.]

BARISTA. You never did say why you're here.

ANDREW SAULTERS. No, sure didn't. Aren't we all trying to figure that out?

B. No. No, it's just you.

Confessions and Well-Wishes

Many of the titles in *No, It's Just You* lift phrases from various writers and performers. Meanwhile, some titles may appear to reference published works or performers, but the connection is incidental. Refer to the following page for a BINGO game on this theme.

Resemblance of any character to any person living or dead is entirely intentional but also hopefully unintelligible. Andrew Saulters thanks his collaborators, wherever they are.

The Most Dangerous Game

Connect five authors in a row to the phrases lifted (or NOT) from their œuvres! Answers are available on the website of Scuppernong Books.

	B	I	N	G	O
1	Rainer Maria Rilke	Pythagoras	Mircea Eliade	NOT Hannah Arendt	Jean-Jacques Rousseau
2	Sheryl Crow	R.P. Blackmur	Peter Handke	Harold Bloom	Plato
3	NOT Thomas J. Fleming	John Ball	Judith Butler	Jonathan Kozol	Theodor W. Adorno
4	Roland Barthes (1973)	Wallace Stevens	William Empson	Horace	NOT Dent May
5	Michel Foucault	NOT Jim Shepard	Walter Benjamin	Matt Damon & Ben Affleck	Roland Barthes (1967)

CPSIA information can be obtained
at www.ICGtesting.com
Printed in the USA
LVHW020000231121
704135LV00009B/1942